SHIPS IN FOCUS BY CARRIER THE ___ 2001

SHIPS IN FOCUS BY CARRIER THE ___ 2001

CAPE TOWN SHIPPING

Ships at Cape Town from 1862–2000

The arrival of Holland Africa's liner *Randfontein* (1958/13,694 grt) on her maiden voyage in 1959. (AN)

CAPE TOWN SHIPPING

Ships at Cape Town from 1862-2000

by
Peter Newall

Published by
Black Dog Press

This book is dedicated to my mother Steffi Newall (1920-1972)
whose love and understanding remains an inspiration

By the same author:
Cape Town Harbour - 1652 to the present
Union-Castle Line - a fleet history

Published by

Blackdog Press

Dorset House, Dorset Street, Blandford Forum, Dorset DT11 7RF, Great Britain

ISBN 0-9539391-0-3 First published 2000
British Library Cataloguing for Publication Data
A Catalogue Record of this book is available from the British Library

Artwork production by Peter Newall
Printed by The Amadeus Press, Cleckheaton, Yorkshire

INTRODUCTION

Cape Town is without doubt one of the world's most beautiful cities. Surrounded by the sea and situated at the base of Table Mountain, the city looks stunning, whatever the time of year. The light is also perfect for photography and for the past 150 years, photographers have excelled in their images of ships at Cape Town. This book is as much a tribute to these photographers as it is a celebration of ships at Cape Town. In choosing the photographs for the book, I have attempted to show not only the variety of ships which called at the Cape, but also a selection of photographs which are a pleasure to view.

Housed in the former Roeland Street Gaol, the Cape Town Archives has a magnificent photographic collection covering a wide range of subjects and includes some beautiful photographs of ships taken by Dr. C. F. Juritz in the 1890s. The Juritz family lived at Sea Point and were great ship lovers. The Archives also own the 10,000-negative Elliott Collection which belonged to the American-born photographer Arthur Elliott (1870-1938). Although Elliott took most of the photographs in the collection, including many architectural shots of old Cape buildings, most of the pre-1900 photos came from other photographers. The amateur photographer Martin Leendertz (1882-1962) was aged six when his family moved from Holland to South Africa. From an early age his interest in ships grew and his photographs taken between the Boer War and the 1930s, although variable in quality, provide a unique record of Cape Town shipping during this period. His collection was left to the Ship Society of South Africa and was recently transferred to the South African Library to become part of their large photographic collection.

For over 20 years Robert Moffat Scott was among the most prolific ship photographers in Cape Town. One of the founders of the Cape Town branch of the World Ship Society, which later became the Ship Society of South Africa, Robert died prematurely in 1959 running to photograph a ship at A-berth. His negatives were sold and were incorporated into major shipping collections such as the Alex Duncan Collection. Many of the published photographs of ships taken at Cape Town between the 1930s and the 1950s are more than likely to have been taken by this larger than life man. John Marsh (1914-1996), on the other hand, ensured that his collection was left to the South African nation and is now owned by the South African Maritime Museum in Cape Town. A contemporary of Scott, John Marsh was one of the few photographer allowed into the Cape Town docks during World War Two and his collection contains many remarkable images of the most famous ships of the day.

Included in the book are a series of pictures taken by two photographers who were interested as much in the atmosphere of the harbour as the ships. My father, Albert Newall (1920-1989), was a leading artist and photographer in the 1950s and 1960s. Most of his photographs were taken with a plate camera and those used in his book *Images of the Cape* now belong to the National Gallery of South Africa. George Aschman (1906-1987) was Managing Editor of the Cape Times and his beautiful photographs of dockside scenes are a tribute to a perfect Cape gentleman.

From the 1960s onwards a new generation of photographers emerged and Ian Shiffman and Robert Pabst are probably the most well known - Robert for the quality of his photographs and Ian for the variety of the images he has taken, many of which have been published under the Table Bay Underway banner. Among the new young shipping photographers, there can be little doubt that Ocean Images Cape Town's Andrew Ingpen, son of South Africa's leading maritime historian Brian Ingpen, is one of the best and his pictures have started appearing world-wide in the leading shipping journals.

The generosity and help I received in preparing this book was overwhelming and I would like to thank Marian George, Assistant Director Cape Town Archives Repository, for the use of photographs in the collection; Denise Crous, Curator of the South African Maritime Museum, for unlimited access to the Marsh Collection; Ian Shiffman, Robert Pabst and Andrew Ingpen for providing a huge selection of photographs to choose from; the Ship Society of South Africa for use of the Leendertz Collection; David Aschman for his generous help with his father's photographs and to Judy, as ever, for helping select the photographs. The quality of reproduction has been helped immeasurably by the excellent prints produced by Peter Jeftha, Pam Warne and Ambrose Greenway. Thanks also to Bill Schell, Bill Laxon, Brian Ingpen and Anthony Cooke for meticulously checking the text; Rear Admiral Roger Morris for information on warships, John Naylon for his expert advise on sailing ships and Earl Sheck for the identification of the crew on *Alabama*.

In brackets, for each ship mentioned, is the year of completion followed by the gross tonnage (grt) for merchant ships or displacement tonnage (dt) for warships. An index and list of photographic sources can be found on page 112.

The Italian liner *Neptunia* (1950/12,838 grt) at East Pier in the 1950s. (GA)

THE DEVELOPMENT OF CAPE TOWN HARBOUR

Despite the strategic importance of the Cape route, it is surprising that Cape Town has only had an enclosed dock since 1870 and a harbour to match its status as a major world port, only in 1943.

Alfred Dock

The first harbour - Alfred Dock, known nowadays as the Alfred Basin - was designed by the foremost harbour engineer in England John (later Sir John) Coode and took ten years to complete. Prince Alfred, second son of Queen Victoria, officiated not only at the start of construction in 1860 but also at the official opening on July 11, 1870.

The Alfred Dock has the unique distinction of being the only dock in Cape Town to have been excavated out of the shoreline rock. The site chosen was around the Chavonnes Battery which was recently uncovered during building work at East Quay. The rock scooped out of the basin provided material for the first breakwater - when the basin was completed the sea was let in. The Alfred Dock entrance with the Gothic-style Clock Tower is called The Cut - see page 32 - and this inner harbour also includes the Robinson Graving Dock which was completed in 1882 - see page 34.

Victoria Basin

In 1883, Sir John Coode proposed a new outer harbour which would add 64 acres to the enclosed water area and some 5,000 feet in extra quayage. The plans also included an outer entrance 250-feet wide, an East Pier 800-feet long and a 2,000-feet South Pier parallel to the Breakwater which would be doubled in length with a cant to the north east. The stone for the new dock came from a site south west of the Alfred Dock - this quarry can be clearly seen in the photographs opposite and was the major source of material for the new docks. From the 1920's until recently the quarry was used for oil storage tanks and is now a yacht marina. Work on the Victoria Basin took from 1889 until 1905 and apart from minor changes, the Alfred Dock and Victoria Basin remained little changed for almost 100 years.

Duncan Dock and the modern harbour

In 1922 work started on a major upgrading of the harbour including the widening of South Pier, later renamed South Arm, the extension of the breakwater by 1,500 feet, a new grain elevator at Collier Jetty and a new basin south east of the Victoria Basin with a new quaywall and three new berths (B to D Berths) on the opposite side of the widened South Arm. The far side of the basin was protected by a random block mole built of huge blocks of concrete. Expansion to the south east was restricted by the Cape Town's popular 1,000 feet-Municipal Pier.

The new basin was not a success - see page 107 - and in 1937, proposals were put forward for a true world-class harbour - the Duncan Dock. The Municipal Pier was demolished and a new mile long quay (E to L Berths) was built on the south east axis, reaching almost to the opposite side of the Bay. Running parallel to the new quay was a long mole, the Eastern Mole. The 15 million cubic yards of sand and mud dredged from the basin was used to form a 360-acre site of reclaimed land in front of the city called the Foreshore. The work on the Duncan Dock took place between 1937 and 1943. The giant Sturrock Dry Dock, the largest in the Southern Hemisphere, was also completed in 1945.

Cape Town Harbour was further modernised between 1969 and 1977 with the building of the Ben Schoeman deep-sea container dock. The extent of the modern Cape Town Harbour can be seen in this aerial view of Cape Town which also shows the city below Table Mountain and the mountain range extending southwards along the Cape Peninsula. (IS)

Alfred Dock and Victoria Basin circa 1905

Alfred Dock and Victoria Basin now (RP)

Ship repairs

Ship repairs have always been an important aspect of Cape Town shipping, especially after the Great Gale of May 17, 1865, the worst ever to hit Cape Town. Eighteen ships were wrecked then and sixty lives lost - above (CA:E8007).

Possibly damaged in that storm was this small clipper barque of the late 1850s or 1860s being repaired on the slipway just north of the Amsterdam Battery, which is visible in the background. The vessel appears to have suffered collision damage as her bulwarks are smashed on the starboard bow - below (CA:E6135).

Right - having lost her rudder and steering gear in a gale, the paddle steamer *Coonanbara* (1862/900 grt) put into Cape Town at the beginning of November 1862 for repairs. Built at Millwall on the River Thames for the New South Wales coastal and river service she was on her delivery voyage from London to Sydney. Fortunately a new slipway had recently been completed and after almost two months she was able to continue her journey. This is probably the earliest photograph of a named ship taken in South Africa. (CA:E6126).

The last days of sail

Long after the introduction of efficient steam-powered ships, sailing vessels continued to ply the world's trades carrying bulk cargoes such as guano, grain and coal for which speed was not essential but cost an important consideration. Seen here in ballast and shortening sail, the four-masted barque *Samaritan* (1891/2,143 grt) was a tramp bulk carrier of the latter days of sail. Originally Canadian-owned, in 1915 she was sold to a Swedish owner and renamed *Dagmar*. On November 11, 1915 she sailed with a crew of 24 from Glasgow bound for Gothenburg on her first voyage under the Swedish flag. She never arrived and became the largest Swedish sailing vessel to go missing. (CA:Holland 37)

This photo taken by Dr. Juritz in January 1894 shows the steel four-masted barque *Conishead* (1892/2,526 grt) lying in the bay after a fast passage from Barrow-in-Furness - her run from Barrow to the Equator of 14 days 8 hours was never beaten by a sailing ship. On August 29, 1917 as *Cooroy* and bound for Liverpool with a cargo of nitrates she was torpedoed off the coast of Ireland by the German submarine *UC 75* and sank. (CA:DRJ714)

Kirkcudbrightshire (1884/1,582 grt) was a well-known iron full-rigger built on the Clyde for the Glasgow "Shire" Line. Soon after arriving in the Alfred Dock, probably in 1898, she is drying her sails with the mainyard cock-billed to clear the wharf installations. She and her sister *Clackmannanshire* lasted until the early 1920s. (CA:J6816)

Lawhill and *Brutus*

Lawhill (1892/2,942 grt) was among the last of the windjammers. A steel four-masted barque she was built for the Dundee ship owner Charles Barrie for the Calcutta jute trade and in 1917 was sold to Captain Gustaf Erikson from Mariehamn in Finland who built up a fleet of some of the most famous sailing ships in the world. With Finland on the side of Germany in World War Two *Lawhill* was seized by the South African Government in 1941 and they operated her between South Africa and Australia manned mainly by South Africans. After the war she languished in Lourenço Marques and was eventually broken up in 1957. Her figurehead was a woman in a long white dress with flowers in her hair and reputedly represented Charles Barrie's daughter. (CA:J3904)

Right - one of the most astonishing survivors of the sailing era lies in Prince Olav Harbour, South Georgia. *Brutus* (1883/1,620 grt) was built as the three-masted steel full-rigged ship *Sierra Pedrosa* and in August 1889 with a cargo of coal, she stranded on Woodstock beach during one of the infamous Cape north-westerly winter gales. On that occasion, she was refloated, but when, thirteen years later almost to the day, she went aground in the same spot, as the newly-named *Brutus*, she was not so lucky - top right. (CA:E8658) This time, she was severely damaged and was later salvaged to become a cold store hulk in Table Bay. In 1917, she was bought by Southern Whaling & Sealing, which at that time was managed by Irvin & Johnson, a local Cape Town fishing firm. In February 1918, she arrived at their South Georgia base Prince Olav Harbour, towed by the catchers *Truls* and *Traveller*. Until the closure of the station in 1931, she served as a coal hulk. This remarkable view of *Brutus* was taken in 1987 by George Mortimore who was Chief Officer of the Royal Fleet Auxiliary *Sir Lancelot,* which can be seen in the background.

13

Two unusual visitors in the 1860s

Over the years Cape Town has seen many of the largest ships of their day. Isambard Kingdom Brunel's *Great Eastern* (1857/18,915 grt) was one of these and although she was a spectacular failure as a passenger ship her size was not surpassed for over forty years until the arrival of White Star's *Celtic* in 1901. After a short career as a transatlantic liner she became a cable-layer in 1865 and laid the first usable telegraph cable across the Atlantic. On December 22, 1869 she arrived in Table Bay en route to Bombay where she was to lay a cable between there and Aden. After an ignominious period as an exhibition ship, *Great Eastern* was sold for demolition on the Mersey in 1889. (CA:M771)

Great Eastern was broken up near the Laird's shipyard at Birkenhead which built two ships well known in South African waters - the troopship *HMS Birkenhead* which was wrecked in 1852 with great loss of life at Danger Point (near Cape Agulhas) and Union-Castle Line's *Windsor Castle*, the largest ever passenger mailship on the South African run. From the same yard came the infamous American Civil War Confederate raider *Alabama* (1862/1,050 grt) which was completed under false pretences as a merchant ship *Enrica*. Armed in the Azores and renamed *Alabama* she roamed the oceans in search of Yankee prey. By the time she was sunk near Cherbourg in July 1864 by *USS Kearsarge* she had captured or destroyed 69 ships. Two years earlier, on August 5, 1862, she arrived in Cape Town in pursuit of the barque *Sea Bride*. The citizens of Cape Town lined the shore to get a good view of the action and during her short stay many visited the ship. In the Cape Town Archives are two photographs taken on board - opposite top is looking aft at the funnel and flying bridge with members of the crew. (CA:AG13079). Below we can see Lieutenants Arthur Sinclair (left) and Richard F. Armstrong standing alongside one of the ship's guns. (CA:AG13081). The visit of *Alabama* lives forever in Cape Town with the celebrated folk song "daar kom die Aliebama" ("there comes the Alabama") which was written soon after the event.

Around the world sailors with a difference

Towards the end of December 1898 the tiny thirty-six foot wooden sloop *Spray* sailed into the Alfred Dock. At the helm was the American adventurer Captain Joshua Slocum who was nearing the end of his epic three-year 46,000-mile solo voyage around the world, the first man to circumnavigate the globe single-handed. During his three month stay in South Africa Slocum toured the country giving lectures whilst *Spray* remained in the care of the harbour authorities. In Pretoria he was introduced to President Kruger who informed him that he could not possibly be travelling around the world but "in the world", as the world was flat! Despite his fame, Captain Slocum was never long in port and in November 1909 he set sail from Rhode Island in *Spray* and was never seen again. (CA:DRJ733)

At the opposite end of the spectrum from *Spray* was the famous steam yacht *Sunbeam* (1874/334 grt) which was owned by the British railway magnate Lord Brassey who twice sailed her around the world but unlike Slocum had a crew of 29 including four stewards and three stewardess/nurses. In 1895 she called at the Cape on her way to Australia where Lord Brassey became Governor of Victoria. As a member of the Royal Yacht Squadron she was allowed to fly the Royal Navy ensign which can be seen on her stern. By the time she was handed over as an Indian hospital ship in 1916 Lord Brassey had completed over half a million miles in her and she was eventually scrapped in 1929.

The docks were overflowing during the Boer War with ships double-banked (CA:E9335)

The Anglo-Boer War

When the Peace of Vereeniging was signed on May 31, 1902 the Anglo-Boer War was finally over. For the British public there was little to celebrate. This war which should have been over "by teatime" dragged on for over two and a half years and cost £200 million and 20,000 British lives. The lack of planning by the anonymous bureaucrats of Whitehall and the numerous blunders of the Army generals had been the source of great embarrassment for the nation and added considerably to the final tally of those wounded and killed. With the deaths of 28,000 Boer women and children and 14,000 Africans in the infamous concentration camps, the image of Britain abroad was also dented forever.

The logistical problems of fighting a war so far from home were horrendous. Between July 1899 and December 1902 chartered ships carried 609,400 troops to and from South Africa at a total cost of £14.7 million. In addition, over a quarter of a million horses and one hundred thousand mules were shipped to the battle zone. In South Africa, Cape Town was the only harbour, which was capable of landing troops and equipment directly from large ships onto the quayside and vessels had to wait weeks in the roadstead before entering the harbour. For ship enthusiasts like Martin Leendertz in Cape Town, however, this was a unique opportunity to see a multitude of vessels, some of which were the most famous ships of the day.
(CA:E9335)

Lake Manitoba (1901/9,674) was less than a year old when she was chartered for five months as an infantry Transport No. 23 in May 1902. Boer War troop transports usually had numbers painted on their sides although many of these changed so they are not a foolproof means of identification. She was one of two passenger ships built by Swan, Hunter for Elder Dempster's Beaver Line Liverpool-Montreal service. In 1903 the Canadian Pacific Railway Company entered the North Atlantic trade and bought Elder Dempster's Canadian services, including *Lake Manitoba* and fourteen other vessels - although she survived World War One she was sold for demolition in 1924. (ML)

A typical scene of chaos in Cape Town's nearly completed outer harbour, Victoria Basin. Here we have another brand-new four-masted Canadia: passenger ship in 1902 - Allan Line's *Ionian* (1901/8,265 grt). Allan was Canadian Pacific's great rival across the Atlantic before they too were take: over by the giant railroad company in 1909. In October 1917 *Ionian* sank near Milford Haven after hitting a mine laid by the German mine-layir submarine *UC 51*. (ML)

ring her three year charter *Orotava* (1889/5,851 grt) carried over 26,000 personnel including Lord Kitchener and General French who are on board as she parts from Cape Town, her funnels belching thick black smoke. Designed as a passenger ship for Pacific Steam Navigation's Liverpool-Valparaiso service, e was transferred after a few voyages to the London-Australia run operated by Orient Line. In 1896 she capsized at Tilbury but was later raised and repaired. ring World War One she was bought by the Admiralty, converted into an armed merchant cruiser and after a brief period as a troopship was scrapped in 23. (ML)

British India Steam Navigation Company's *Golconda* (1888/6,037 grt) was an elegantly designed one-off. Built on speculation by the Sunderland shipyard William Doxford & Sons to show off their skills during a period of global recession, she was bought by British India for the London-Calcutta service. For fifteen years she was the largest ship in the BI fleet. Used briefly as an infantry transport during the latter part of the Boer War, in 1913 she was transferred to the East African route. Two years later she became an Indian Expeditionary Force transport and in this role she was sunk by a mine off the Suffolk Coast with the loss of nineteen lives. (ML)

As well as troop transports, many ships were fitted out as cavalry transports whilst others carried only mules or horses. With the guerrilla tactics of the Boers the British had to chase the enemy over long distances and this required large numbers of horses. As the war progressed the death toll among the animals was appalling. Poor planning meant that many were sent to the front without any rest from the strenuous sea journey and succumbed to disease or starvation. Whilst 75,000 horses left England with the cavalry, only 2,400 returned. Originally built as a transatlantic cattle carrier with a flush deck, to accommodate horses, William Johnston's *Maplemore* (1899/7,803 grt) was fitted with an extra deck, which gave her a top-heavy appearance. As well as carrying cavalry regiments from England *Maplemore* also conveyed Austrian horses on two voyages from Fiume to Cape Town. After her Boer War service she was sold to John Ellerman's newly acquired City Line and renamed *City of Edinburgh*. Surviving a torpedo attack in 1915 she was demolished in 1929. (ML)

The primitive loading conditions at Cape Town are evident in this photograph of a Boer War troop transport. The ship is probably one of the fleet of the City Line which until the 1901 take-over by Ellerman had been controlled by the Smith family whose "City" ships had been well known on the Indian subcontinent for over fifty years. (ML)

Two former crack transatlantic liners nearing the end of their days were also used as Boer War troop transports. Although tiny by today's standards *Aurania* (7,269 grt) was one of the world's largest ships when completed for Cunard Line in 1883 - her passenger capacity was 500 first and 700 steerage. Chartered for three years she carried over 30,000 troops to and from South Africa and was scrapped in 1905. (ML)

Cunard's great rival on the Atlantic was White Star Line and in the early 1870s the company ordered from Harland & Wolff two new liners - *Britannic* (1874/5,004 grt) and *Germanic* (1875/5,008 grt) - their largest ships to that date. They were also record breakers and *Britannic* reduced the Atlantic crossing times in both directions to less than 7.5 days. Soon after the end of her Boer War contract she was sold to German breakers and towed for demolition at Hamburg in 1903. Her sister was purchased by the Turkish Government in 1910 and lasted until 1950. (ML)

On September 1, 1900 after the defeat of the Boers by the armies of Lord Roberts and General Sir Redvers Buller the Transvaal Republic became the British colony of Transvaal. On October 24, 1900 Buller left Cape Town on *Dunvegan Castle* (1896/5,958 grt) for a hero's welcome in England. The British glory was short-lived, however, as a vicious guerrilla campaign ensued which extended the war for another year and a half. (CA:DRJ945)

The scourge of the British Empire. Boer prisoners-of-war showing off their wooden carvings. In the end the Boers were triumphant when the Union of South Africa was formed in 1910 with a former Boer General Louis Botha appointed the first Prime Minister. (CA:AG2525)

A very unusual visitor to Cape Town - the Rotterdam-London cross channel steamer *Batavier VI* (1903/1,181 grt) which was owned by Wm. H. Müller & Co. This photograph taken on November 30, 1904 (ML) shows her with flags at half mast and a crowd gathered around her stern area. The reason for this is apparent below (CA:AG1124) with the ship's crew (note the Wm. H. Müller & Co. insignia on their garments) preparing to take a coffin draped in the Transvaal Republic flag ashore - this contained the body of President Kruger who died in exile on July 14 at Clarens on the shore of Lake Geneva and was buried in Pretoria on December 16, 1904. *Batavier VI* was sold for service between Gibraltar and North Africa in 1929 and ended her career stranded near Cape Spartel in June 1940.

The extraordinary *HMS Penelope*

After France ordered the first sea-going iron clad warship *Gloire* in 1858, the British Admiralty responded with the iron hulled *Warrior* and *Black Prince* and plans were made to significantly increase the ironclad fleet. The armed corvette *HMS Penelope* (4,470 dt) was the last of a series of wooden-hulled ironclads and the first large Royal Navy vessel to have twin screws and twin rudders - the screws could be lifted out of the water to reduce drag whilst under sail. Despite all this modern development the fancy stern windows, a hangover from the 18th century, remained - above. (CA:G470).

HMS Penelope saw action at the bombardment of Alexandria in 1882 and six years later was sent to Simon's Town as a floating barracks and remained there for the next 25 years. In 1896 she was paid off and became a prison hulk and during the Boer War was used extensively to house Boer prisoners-of-war prior to their exile abroad. In 1912 she was bought by a local businessman who sold her in turn to shipbreakers in Genoa. The famous William Watkins tug *Oceana* (1889/337 grt) was hired to make the tow to Italy. On arrival at Simon's Town from England the captain of *Oceana* was dissatisfied with the condition of *HMS Penelope* but he managed to tow her to Cape Town where she arrived in a very leaky state in 1913 and the tow was abandoned - opposite top (ML). A more powerful tug was then chartered, this time from the Dutch firm Smit. Despite some initial difficulty *Roode Zee* (1908/573 grt), the mast of which can be seen to the left of *HMS Penelope*, managed to complete the tow to Genoa in thirty-four days - opposite below. (CA:E3354).

Union-Castle mailships

No story of Cape Town shipping would be complete without mention of the ships of the Union-Castle Line, which carried mail between Britain and South Africa for 120 years. Prior to the formation of the Union-Castle Mail Steamship Company in 1900 Union Line and Castle Packets shared the mail contract and were deadly rivals. The latter was very old-fashioned and continued to operate with auxiliary sail right into the late 1890s. In this April 1899 photograph (above: CA:DRJ768) sails are evident on the foremast of the Mauritius intermediate *Doune Castle* (1890/4,046 grt) whilst below is an early view of *Grantully Castle* (1879/3,489 grt) leaving Cape Town with men unfurling the sails. (CA:AG1813)

In the 1890s both mail companies tried to outdo each other with ever-improved and larger ships. Castle Line was first off the mark in 1890 with the largest liner built for the South African run, *Dunottar Castle* (1890/5,465 grt). (CA:DRJ1049)

Dunottar Castle was soon surpassed by the magnificent *Scot* and a series of handsome Union liners from Harland & Wolf of which *Briton* (1897/10,248 grt) was a perfect example. (CA:S84)

The great Scot

One of the most beautiful mailships. Union Line's *Scot* (1891/6,844 grt) was the first twin-screw Cape liner and her March 1893 Southampton-Cape Town record of 14 days 18 hours 57 minutes remained unbroken for 43 years. Despite lengthening in 1896, which considerably enhanced her appearance, she remained a failure because of her high operating cost, and limited cargo capacity. In 1905 she was sold to the German line HAPAG and became the cruiseship *Oceana*.

Here are four views of this unique liner. When she first appeared (above CA:S18) she was painted black but this was soon changed to white - opposite top (CA:G806) - note the scrollwork on her bow, the "lighthouse" containing the starboard light and the smart hansom cabs on the quayside, a far cry from the taxis of today. In 1896 *Scot* was cut in half and lengthened by 54 feet - here she is leaving Cape Town sometime after 1900 in Union-Castle colours - below (ML). The slim lines of the clipper bow - opposite below (ML) show why the ship was able to make such good speed. Unfortunately her coal consumption was extremely high and she never paid her way for Union Line.

In September 1936, *Stirling Castle* (1936/25,550 grt) shattered *Scot*'s 43-year-old southbound record. With the construction of the new dock (later called the Duncan Dock) well underway, she and her sister, *Athlone Castle* (1936/25,564 grt), were the last mailships whose length was restricted by the dimensions of the Victoria Basin. It was a credit to the skills of the pilots and tugboat men that these ships were able to be manoeuvred in such tight spaces, as this 1930s photograph shows.

After the war the 4pm Friday mailship departure from A-berth in the Duncan Dock was a familiar sight for many Capetonians - here *Edinburgh Castle* (1948/28,705 grt) leaves for the UK. (GA)

The photographer Terrence McNally took some of the finest photographs of Union-Castle liners in Cape Town - many were aerial views like this one of *Kenya Castle* (1952/17,041 grt) in the 1950s which was probably taken by him. Unfortunately since his death a few years ago his negatives have been dispersed and their whereabouts are unknown. *Kenya Castle* is the last of the trio built for the Round Africa service to survive - she is currently laid up in Greece as *Amerikanis*.

The excellent night-time shot by Robert Pabst shows another survivor of the Union-Castle fleet - *Transvaal Castle* (1961/32,697 grt) - which later became Safmarine's *S.A Vaal* and, until the recent demise of Premier Cruises, operated weekly sailing from Houston to Mexico as *Big Red Boat III*.

The Cut

The Cut is the entrance to the Alfred Dock, the first manmade harbour in South Africa, officially opened on July 11, 1870 by Queen Victoria's son Prince Alfred, Duke of Edinburgh. Until the recent installation of the footbridge, The Cut remained virtually unchanged for over 100 years with the 1883-built Time and Tide Gauge House or Clock Tower the most important building in the Alfred Dock complex - here the Port Captain had his office before he moved to the new building on the opposite side of The Cut in 1904 which is now the headquarters of the Victoria & Alfred Waterfront Company. (AI)

On a misty day at the turn of the 20th century a photographer is setting up his camera with the Clock Tower and the long-gone flagstaff flying the flags of well known shipping lines such as Clan, Bucknall and Union. (CA:G819)

Tied alongside The Cut is *Wladimir Sawin* (1898/2,058 grt) owned by a Danish company which traded with Russia (A/S Det Dansk Russiske DS), hence the Russian name. She had an extraordinary long life and was only broken up in 1953 as the Finnish-owned *Parma*. (ML)

Co-incidentally, *Raglan Castle* (1897/4,324 grt) berthed in the same spot was sold to a Danish company which chartered her briefly as a Russian troopship in 1906. This photograph was probably taken in 1903 and also shows building work on both the North Quay Warehouse (now the Victoria & Alfred Hotel) and the Port Captain's Office with the Union-Castle Line passenger tender *Natal* (1892/158 grt) alongside. (CA:AG947)

Robinson Graving Dock

Opened by the Governor of the Cape, Sir Hercules Robinson, in 1882 the Robinson Graving Dock is probably one of the oldest commercial dry-docks still in regular use - the dock also contains the bench mark for sea level in South Africa. (PN)

In for repairs - Bullard King's Natal Line steamer *Umsinga* (1901/2,963 grt). A cargo ship with space for 32 passengers her regular trade was between London and Natal, she and her sister *Umvolosi* lasted until the late 1920s. (ML)

Ionic (1883/4,753 grt) was one of four large cargo carriers ordered by White Star Line from Harland & Wolff. A beautifully balanced ship, in 1884 she was placed on the joint Shaw Savill & Albion-White Star service between England and Australia and New Zealand and fitted with refrigerated space for 750 tons of frozen meat. In February 1893, nearing the Cape, her propeller shaft snapped and she was towed into Cape Town by the Castle liner *Hawarden Castle* (1883/4,241 grt). This photograph was most likely taken during her lengthy stay in Cape Town for repairs. In 1900 she was sold to Aberdeen Line as *Sophocles* and is featured again on page 61. (CA:DRJ690)

Hawarden Castle can be seen dressed overall in 1885 at North Quay behind the Robinson Graving Dock with *Taymouth Castle* (1877/1,827 grt). (CA:E8204)

Coaling

Before World War One most ships were coal-fired and Cape Town, as now, was an important refuelling stop. The coal sheds were situated next to the Collier Jetty where barges were loaded with coal and towed to the ships in the harbour - here we see *Ingoma* (1913/5,686 grt) with two coal barges alongside. After the First World War, many ships started using oil instead of coal and in 1923 a grain elevator was erected at the Collier Jetty although the name remains to this day. *Ingoma* was the only passenger ship ordered for the Harrison-Rennie Line South African service. Later transferred to the London-West Indies run she was sold in 1937 to Italian owners and as *San Giovanni Battista* was severely damaged by British aircraft on a voyage from Italy to Tripoli in 1942. (ML)

Coaling was a very dirty business, especially for passenger ships, and every effort had to be made to prevent coal dust entering the passenger accommodation. Awnings were used to cover most areas, as can be seen on White Star Line's *Ceramic* (1913/18,481 grt), which at one time was the largest ship on the Cape route. In November 1942, *Ceramic* met a tragic end when she exploded after being torpedoed west of the Azores with the loss of all but one of her 656 passengers and crew. (ML)

World War One

At the beginning of August 1914 war was declared between Britain and Germany and Cape Town once again saw a flurry of activity. In the same month a number of German vessels were seized as prizes of war including the Deutsche Ost-Afrika-Linie steamer *Rufidji* (1911/ 5,442 grt) which was captured off Cape Point. For the British Government one of the early objectives of the war was the conquest of the German African colonies and *Rufidji* was soon put into service as a troopship - here troops for the German South West Africa campaign are preparing to board the ship at South Pier. She later became *Huntscliff* under Union-Castle management and in October 1918 foundered in the Atlantic after encountering rough weather. (CA:AG14060)

P&O's *Karmala* (1914/8,983 grt) also played an important role in the Africa campaign. As a brand-new cargo-passenger liner, in November 1914 she became the headquarters for the Indian Expeditionary Force during the landings at Tanga, East Africa. She survived the war and was sold to Japanese breakers in 1932. (ML)

Because of a shortage of ships during the war the intermediate Round Africa Union-Castle liner *Llanstephan Castle* (1914/ 11,293 grt) was transferred to the UK-South Africa mail service. To avoid detection by enemy ships her hull was painted black but not too effectively as the bow wake appears to have washed away much of the paint work at the base of her bow. Tied alongside is the veteran South African coaster *Nautilus* (1890/360 grt) which operated between Cape Town and Port Nolloth on the Cape western coast - she was lost in 1919 off Possession Island whilst on charter to a diamond syndicate. (ML)

For most of the war *Kenilworth Castle* (1904/12,974 grt) remained on the mail service and was painted an all over grey. Replaced by *Stirling Castle*, in 1937 she was sent to breakers in Northumberland. (ML)

Just before the war Norddeutscher Lloyd ordered a dozen large freighters for their Bremen-Australia route - all had very tall kingposts with ventilator tops. One of these was *Pfalz* (1913/6,570 grt) which was seized at the outset of war in Melbourne. Converted into a troopship by the Commonwealth of Australia, she was renamed *Boorara* (seen here) - her career ended in 1937 when as the Greek *Nereus* she was wrecked on Vancouver Island. (ML)

The tiny vessel behind the Danish cargo ship *Kina* (1911/4,714 grt) was one of the most famous merchant ships in World War One - *Lodorer* (1904/3,207 grt). Between 1915 and 1917 she was *Farnborough* but her real identity was *Q5* under the command of Commander Gordon Campbell. Q-ships were merchant ships with hidden guns used as decoys to attract German submarines. Commander Campbell was awarded the Victoria Cross when his ship, despite being hit and sinking, opened fire and sank *U 83* off the Irish coast. Campbell's message to the Admiralty after the event was "*Q5* slowly sinking respectfully wishes you good-bye." The ship was, however, refloated and once again became a regular merchant ship - she was broken up in 1928. (ML)

Warships

Cape Town has long been known as the *Tavern of the Seas* and the visit of warships has always generated a special sense of excitement not only for Capetonians who are renowned for their hospitality but also for the crew. The British cruiser *HMS Good Hope* (1902/14,150 dt) visited Cape Town twice in the years following the Boer War - the first time, in 1903, was with Joseph Chamberlain, Secretary for the Colonies and she is seen here during that visit at No.4 Berth South Pier. (ML)

Her next visit was for the National Convention in November 1908. On that occasion she was the flagship of a special squadron under Rear Admiral Sir Percy Scott and was berthed at the Loch Jetty, which was removed in 1921. Thousands flocked to the ship and no doubt gazed in awe at the 9.2-inch gun on her forecastle, which with the rest of her guns was no match against the German armoured cruisers *Scharnhorst* and *Gneisenau* which sank her with all hands in the Battle of Coronel, Chile on November 1, 1914. (CA:E8074)

Happier times - *Good Hope* dressed overall and flying a rear admiral's flag to celebrate King's Day November 9, 1908. (Left CA:DRJ607 and below CA:DRJ611)

Warships lit at night, always an impressive sight. *HMS Carnarvon* (left) at the Elbow and *HMS Antrim* at No. 4 South Pier were part of a trio of *Devonshire*-class armoured cruisers which accompanied *HMS Good Hope* in 1908. (CA:AG14935)

In January ten years earlier, two ships of the Imperial German Navy paid a call - *Habicht* (1879/989 dt) (left) a gunboat and the fourth-rate cruiser *Seeadler* (1892/1,838 dt). They spent most of their active life abroad and are painted in the livery of the German foreign service i.e. white hull and buff upperworks. (CA:DRJ146)

On February 17, 1947 the British Royal Family visited South Africa on the last British-built battleship - the 44,500 dt 1946-built *HMS Vanguard*. Note the four tugs entering Duncan Dock dressed overall whilst the royal cars are kept cool with covers. The outdated *Vanguard* was sold for scrap in 1960 after only 14 years of service.

Queen Elizabeth returned to South Africa forty-eight years later on March 20, 1995 on the Royal Yacht *Britannia* seen passing the Elbow (right) as she enters the Victoria Basin. (RP)

HMS Monarch (8,322 dt) was in active service with the Royal Navy for 33 years - the longest effective life of any of the RN's armoured ships. Built in 1869 she was the first sea-going turret ship i.e. with heavily plated revolving turrets each carrying one or more guns. *HMS Monarch* was also the first British warship fitted with 12-inch guns. She was rebuilt between 1890 and 1897 and is seen here in the Robinson Graving Dock in March 1898 - the gun in her fighting top is for firing at torpedo boats. A guard ship at Simon's Town from 1897 to 1902 she was reduced to a hulk in 1904 and sent home the following year for scrapping. (CA:DRJ999/2)

Like *HMS Monarch*, *HMS Devonshire* (1905/10,850 dt) was built at the Chatham naval dockyard. During Sir Percy Scott's visit in 1908, whilst her two sisters were berthed at South Pier and the Elbow she was alongside No. 2 Jetty. In World War One she operated in the North Sea and on the North America and West Indies Station and was sold for scrap in 1921. (CA:E8076)

In 1937 five giant 40,000 dt-battleships of the *King George V*-class were laid down and completed during 1939 and 1940. *HMS Prince of Wales* was the second in the series and in May 1941, less than two months after her completion, she was seriously damaged in an engagement with the German battleship *Bismarck* during which *HMS Hood* was sunk with the loss of all but 3 of her 1,419 crew. In November 1941 she called at Cape Town on her way to Singapore when this remarkable photograph was taken by John Marsh at A-Berth, Duncan Dock looking down at the camouflaged 14-inch gun barrels. On December 10, 1941 *HMS Prince of Wales* and the 1916-built battlecruiser *HMS Repulse* were both sunk in a Japanese air attack and although 840 men were killed in both ships, 2,081 were rescued. (JM)

Many of the early British aircraft carriers were conversions, like *HMS Eagle* (1920/21,630 dt) which was built using the hull of an incomplete Chilean battleship, hence the dreadnought bow. Painted in disruptive camouflage *HMS Eagle* is seen arriving at Cape Town in May 1941 - note the aircraft homing beacon at the head of her foretopmast and the floats of the anti-torpedo booms at the entrance to Duncan Dock. She was torpedoed and sunk by the German submarine *U 73* on August 11, 1942 with the loss of 160 men during the Malta convoy code-named Operation Pedestal. (JM)

The handsome *Vineta* (1899/6,599 dt) was one of a class of five heavy cruisers built for the German Navy towards the end of the 19th century. She served abroad for the first six years of her career and is seen here in Imperial foreign service livery. Between 1909 and 1911 she was rebuilt and emerged with two funnels and a pole foremast instead of a heavy military foremast - she became an accommodation vessel at Kiel in 1915 and was scrapped in 1920. (ML)

Flying the Japanese Navy ensign during her April 1910 visit, the battlecruiser *Ikoma* (1908/13,750 dt) was one of a Japanese-built pair ordered to replace battleships lost during the Japan-Russia War. In 1919 she became a gunnery training ship but was disarmed three years later under the provisions of the Washington Treaty and sent to the breakers in 1924. (ML)

Unmistakably French with widely spaced pairs of funnels with top hats - *Dupleix* (1903/7,578 dt) was the name ship of a class of three lightly armed cruisers - the largest guns were only 6.4 inches. Left: taken on board whilst berthed at South Pier with an excellent view of her steam launch. (CA:E8082)

The profile shot below shows the crew's washing hanging up to dry, a common feature in all navies before the days of on-board laundry facilities and drying rooms. Like many warships built at the turn of the century, *Dupleix* was scrapped in the early 1920s. (ML)

Built in 1896 the 9,215 dt-cruiser *USS Brooklyn* was a very unusual one-off with an exaggerated tumblehome (clearly shown left) so that the wing gun turrets amidships could have a clear line of fire fore and aft. Her chart house and bridge were built round the foremast. Although she was a Spanish-American War flagship during the 1898 Battle of Santiago, Cuba, she saw no further action during her career, and was demolished in the 1920s. (ML)

A wonderful contrast. Above - smartly dressed Edwardians visiting *USS Brooklyn* (CA:E8087) and - below - three attractive young South Africans in the 1950s gazing at sailors aboard the Gearing-class destroyer *USS Charles H. Roan* (1946/2,425 dt). The Gearing-class consisted of almost 100 ships. *Charles H. Roan* was sold to Turkey in 1973 and as *Maresal Fevzi Cakmak* was broken up in 1995. (GA)

Tugs

Boarding passengers in the Victoria Basin at the turn of the 20th century - the wooden paddle tug *John Paterson* (1882/99 grt) was named after the Cape Parliament MP who drowned on one of the ships which rescued passengers from the stricken Union Line *American* in 1880. Originally based at Port Elizabeth, she was bought by the Table Bay Harbour Board for use as a tender and later became a pleasure steamer. She disappeared with her owner on board in 1906. (CA:E8596)

When she arrived in 1893, the steel-hulled *Alert* (1892/194 grt) was the largest and most powerful tug at Cape Town - here she is towing *Doune Castle* in April 1899. After 16 years of service in Table Bay she was sold to the Townsville Harbour Board, Queensland, Australia in 1909. (CA:DRJ769)

In the 1930s S.A. Railways & Harbours ordered a series of tugs which were among the most powerful in the world. Featuring the name of the well-known Prime Minister of the Cape Colony, *John X. Merriman* (1938/621 grt) was one of five coal-fired tugs built on the Clyde during 1937 and 1938 by Lobnitz & Company. In this photograph taken in 1938 or 1939 she is entering the Victoria Basin probably after assisting *Windsor Castle* or *Arundel Castle* which is sailing in the background. The *Merriman* was withdrawn and scrapped in 1980. (AG)

With *QE2* in the distance, *Danie Hugo* (1959/812 grt) was one of the last South African steam tugs built in Scotland. Oil-burning and like most of the S.A.R. & H. tugs, always in immaculate condition. She had a relatively short career and was scrapped in 1984, only a few years after the 1930s-built tugs went to the breakers. (PN)

Passenger liners in World War Two

John Marsh was one of the few photographer allowed to take pictures in the harbour during the war and his most famous photograph was a panoramic view taken from the top of the Grain Elevator on April 18, 1941 of the largest troopship convoy to visit the Southern Hemisphere. This is a portion of that photograph and shows: Victoria Basin: *Orion* (Orient Line - No. 3 South Arm), *Strathmore* (P&O - No. 4 South Arm); Bay: *Capetown Castle* (Union-Castle); Duncan Dock: *HMS Nelson* (A-berth), *Carnarvon Castle* (Union-Castle - B-berth) and *Duchess of York* (Canadian Pacific - C-berth). (JM)

A month earlier, *Nova Scotia* (1926/6,796 grt) sailed for Suez with troops - note the A-frame on her bow for the deflection of mines. In peacetime she and her sister *Newfoundland* operated as passenger liners for Johnston Warren Lines on their Liverpool-Canada service. On November 28, 1942 she became the worst sea disaster in South African waters when she was torpedoed by the German submarine *U 177* off the Zululand coast. She sank in less than five minutes with the loss of 863 lives, most of whom were Italian prisoners-of-war. (ML)

With her giant funnel and carrying troops for the Middle East, the French liner *Pasteur* (1939/29,253 grt) is being brought alongside E-berth during the visit of the April 1941 convoy. She was completed at the outbreak of war but her maiden voyage from Bordeaux to Buenos Aires was cancelled, and in 1940, she became a troopship managed by Cunard-White Star Line. She never operated on her intended route and was sold in 1957 to Norddeutscher Lloyd who converted her into the transatlantic liner, *Bremen*. After a spell with Chandris Line, she became an accommodation ship in Saudi Arabia and sank on her way to the breakers in 1980. (JM)

For many, the greatest Transatlantic liner was French Line's *Ile de France* (1927/45,153 grt). Her interiors were unlike any seen on an ocean liner before or since and were the height of elegance. For the thousands of troops who travelled in stark accommodation during her six-year stint as a troopship, however, she was probably just another troop carrier. Here she is leaving Duncan Dock with repatriated service personnel in November 1945. She returned to the Le Havre-New York route in 1949 and ten years later was sold to Japan for scrap - her final role was in the film *Last Voyage* in which she was scuttled in shallow waters much to the disgust of her many admirers. (JM)

In 1940 Cape Town also saw the four largest Cunard liners. Because of her size *Aquitania* (1914/45,647 grt) was a troopship in both wars and in March 1940 she called at the Cape without troops on her way to Australia - alongside is a Leaf-class Royal Fleet Auxiliary tanker. *Aquitania* was scrapped in 1950. (JM)

Queen Mary (1936/81,235 grt) arrived in April 1940 from New York bound for Australia where she was to be converted into a 5,000-capacity troopship. Too big for the harbour, she had to anchor in the Bay. (JM)

In February 1940 the nearly-completed largest ship in the world - *Queen Elizabeth* (1940/83,673 grt) - slipped out of the Clyde and headed for New York. In November she left New York for Singapore where she too was to receive a troopship conversion. Her calls at Cape Town included her first major voyage on November 27, 1940 (above) and her final voyage in June 1971 as *Seawise University* (cover) - the name was a play on the initials of her new owner, the Chinese shipping magnate C. Y. Tung. In January 1972 she caught fire at Hong Kong in mysterious circumstances and was destroyed. (JM)

Designed for the London-New York service *Mauretania* (1939/35,739 grt) looked like a smaller version of *Queen Elizabeth*. Her first visit to Cape Town was in May 1940 and she carried many South African troops to and from the Middle East during the war. Here she is leaving Duncan Dock on September 9, 1945 bound for Liverpool with 4,000 service personnel and 1,000 civilians - note the guns on her stern. After the war she was placed on the Southampton-New York route but with increased airline competition across the Atlantic was employed more and more as a cruiseship and was eventually scrapped in 1965. (JM)

Cargo ships

Often overlooked because they do not have the glamour of passenger liners or warships, without them we would not have many of the essential goods in life. They also provide an extraordinary variety of types and usually had very interesting careers.

Founded in 1853, the same year as Union Line, the Liverpool-based Thos. & Jas. Harrison better known as Harrison Line is one of the oldest British shipping lines still in business. *Wanderer* (1891/4,086 grt) was a typical three-island cargo ship of the 1890s with tall fidded masts and open bridge - note also the oil lamp hanging from the forestay. Although small she remained with the company for over 30 years before being sold to Genoese buyers in 1922. (ML)

City of Florence (1918/6,862 grt) stayed with her original owners for an even longer period of time - 38 years. Built by William Gray, West Hartlepool for Hall Line, which was part of John Ellerman's empire, she was sold in 1956 to a Greek company who renamed her *Mount Olympus*. Here she is leaving port in October 1958 - I visited her then as a young boy and the following year she was broken up in Japan.

In the early 1920s DADAG (German-Australian Steamship Company) ordered a large number of ships to replace those lost during the war. Among the group built for the company by Blohm & Voss at Hamburg was *Cassel* (1922/6,047 grt), a turbine-driven cargo liner with space for 18 passengers. A distinctive-looking ship, she had a very short well forward and a counter stern. In 1926 DADAG was taken over by Hamburg America Line (HAPAG) and here she is in HAPAG colours dropping her pilot. In 1940 she was seized by the Dutch - renamed *Mendanau* and managed by Stoomvaart Maatschappij "Nederland". On a voyage from New York to Egypt via Cape Town she was torpedoed and sunk by the German submarine *U 752* with the loss of 69 lives. (ML)

The Bank Line was one of the most successful British cargo lines of the 20th century and the company's founder Andrew Weir, Lord Inverforth, was among the first British cargo ship owners to recognise the importance of the oil engine. In the 1920s he placed an order with Harland & Wolff for 21 vessels, all motorships. Many survived the war and were only broken up in the 1950s. One which did not was *Alynbank* (1925/5,151 grt) and in 1939 she was requisitioned as an anti-aircraft ship and in 1944 sunk off Normandy as part of Gooseberry Harbour which was used during the Normandy Landings. Arriving in the Victoria Basin in the 1930s she has a slight list to port probably caused by cargo shifting or more likely the timber carried on deck. (AD)

The ubiquitous Greek tramp - the Liberty ship was the largest class of standard ships ever built. Between 1941 and 1945 over 2,700 were completed in yards across the United States. One still exists in Cape Town, albeit in pieces - *Thomas T. Tucker* - which was wrecked near Cape Point in November 1942. In the post-war years the Liberty ship was a godsend to ship owners who were unable to obtain new ships because shipyards were fully booked. For the Greeks, however, the Liberty was the foundation of a golden era - 98 were given to Greece and this helped re-establish many Greek companies. One of these was *Eurymedon* (7,250 grt) which was taken over in 1947 - here she is in the late 1950s as *Panagiotis D.* (GA)

Harrison Line owned ten Liberty ships and in the 1950s these were joined by a series of new motorships mainly from the Sunderland shipyard, William Doxford & Sons. *Defender* (1955/8,367 grt) was one of a class of four built between 1955 and 1959 - they were also the last to be ordered with the traditional style of superstructure amidships. In 1975 she was sold to a Panamanian company and renamed *Euromariner* but after suffering an engine breakdown was sold for scrap in 1977. (IS)

Among the regular traders to South Africa in the 1950s arguably the most attractive were those completed for Messageries Maritimes in the mid to late 1950s. With distinctive black funnels they were beautifully balanced ships. Ten ships of this type were built, including *Moonie* (1955/6,936 grt), which was sold in 1976 to a Cypriot buyer. For a brief period she was *Geneva* before being sold to Chinese breakers in 1978. (IS)

From the late 1950s the V-shaped Stülcken heavy lift derricks became as much of a trademark for DDG Hansa as the Maltese cross on the funnel. The Bremen firm was established in 1881, and by the late 1970s, had became a major heavy lift carrier with a fleet of some 70 ships including *Trautenfels* (1974/7,196 grt) which was built in Japan with five other sisters for a Greek company but taken over by Hansa. In 1980, just short of its centenary, the company was declared bankrupt and all its ships sold - *Trautenfels* was bought by a Greek firm and renamed *Trautenbels*. (RP)

Aberdeen White Star Line

George Thompson's Aberdeen Line owned some of the most beautiful sailing ships ever built including the famous clipper *Thermopylae*, the great rival to *Cutty Sark*. The sailing ship tradition was so entrenched in the company that their steamships built between 1881 and 1904 all had elegant clipper bows. Completed in 1899 *Moravian* (4,573 grt) was one of the last square-rigged passenger ships to be built and like the rest of the fleet had a green hull - she carried 50 first class passengers and 650 in third. Superseded by much larger ships on the London-Australia run she was sold in 1914 to a Bombay-based company. Renamed *Akbar*, she was scrapped in 1923. (ML)

In 1891, a year after *Thermopylae* was sold, the name was transferred to a new 3,711 grt-steamship which was constructed by the Hall, Russell & Co. shipyard at Aberdeen. Unlike her namesake which lasted almost 40 years the second *Thermopylae* had a relatively short career - homeward bound from Australia she ran aground in front of the Green Point lighthouse on a moonlit night, September 11, 1899. All on board were rescued including a racehorse belonging to the actress Lily Langtry. For the ship there was no salvation and with the relentless pounding of the Atlantic waves she soon broke up. (CA:DRJ73)

To replace *Thermopylae* Aberdeen Line bought their first steamship with a straight stem - White Star Line's *Ionic* (see page 35) which had an extensive refit in 1894 which included an engine conversion, the heightening of her funnel and the removal of all her yards except on the foremast. Renamed *Sophocles* she served her new owners for six years from 1900 to 1906 before being sold to breakers. Here we see two views of the ship at South Pier - below: baggage is being offloaded from a cart - note the canvas ventilators over the engine room which attempted to bring some relief to those working in the stifling heat of the engine room. (ML)

Mishaps and tragedy

With treacherous seas and variable weather conditions, the Cape coast is littered with wrecks. Rescue in the early days was fraught with difficulties never more so than in the case of Shaw Savill and Albion's cargo ship *Maori* (1893/5,200 grt) which was wrecked at Duiker Point near Llandudno in the early hours of August 4, 1909 in thick fog. The weather was very rough and a number of the crew including the captain were drowned when two of the lifeboats were overwhelmed - one lifeboat managed to reach Hout Bay and a rescue team was sent to the wreck which by now was stern first on the rocks with the ship's forepart submerged. This photograph shows men on the stern and a sole crewmember on the foremast - he later slipped into the sea and drowned. All but one of the thirteen on the stern were eventually rescued and out of a total of 55 crew only 21 survived.

A few miles south of Duiker Point are the soft white sands of Noordhoek Beach. Here high and dry after over 100 years is the wreck of *Kakapo* (1898/1,093 grt) - her sternpost still in place and her intact boiler a testament to Scottish engineering skills. Recently-acquired by the Union Steamship Company of New Zealand *Kakapo* was on her delivery voyage to New Zealand when she mistakenly identified Chapman's Peak as Cape Point and ran aground with no loss of life. This photograph shows her not long after she went ashore. (CA:E8067)

The cargo liner *Vinstra* (1910/4,668 grt), owned by the well known Norwegian line Wilhelm Wilhelmsen, had a narrow escape when she ran aground at Three Anchor Bay in thick fog in April 1922 not far from where *Thermopylae* was wrecked but with the weather calm she was towed off at high tide. Union-Castle's *Gaika* also briefly ran ashore nearby in the same peasouper. *Vinstra* had a long life and was only scrapped in 1958 as the Finnish-owned *Herakles*. (CA:DRJ174)

Not so lucky. After an engine failure, the tiny Dutch-built coaster *Basuto Coast* (1937/246 grt) suffered the indignity of being wrecked opposite the popular Sea Point swimming pool during a winter storm in 1954.

On May 7, 1901 at the end of her voyage from England the Union-Castle liner *Tantallon Castle* (1894/5,636 grt) ran aground in fog on Robben Island, Table Bay. All on board were rescued but despite the efforts of local tugs she remained fast and was declared a constructive total loss. A popular ship, she was the first Castle Line vessel with quadruple expansion engines. (RP)

Seen here during the fruit export season - *Royston Grange* (1959/10,262 grt) was owned by Houlder Bros. and operated on the Britain-South American run carrying frozen meat and dairy produce. On May 11, 1972 en route for London she was in the River Plate in dense fog and despite modern navigation equipment collided with the Chinese tanker *Tien Chee* - the intensity of the fire which followed was so great that all 74 passengers and crew on board *Royston Grange* died instantly whilst eight men on the tanker were also killed – this was one of the worst British maritime disasters in recent years. (RP)

The "Green Goddess" - Cunard Line's *Caronia* (1948/34,172 grt) was a regular caller at the Cape - her first visit to Cape Town was on February 4, 1950 during her Great Africa Cruise from New York. (IS)

Despite her age the former *Vistafjord* now renamed *Caronia* (1973/24,292 grt) remains one of the finest cruise ships afloat. (AI)

Italian design and Swedish style. Swedish American Line's *Gripsholm* (1957/23,191 grt) was one of the world's most elegant liners in the 1950s and her first Cape Town call in February 1959 was spent in the Sturrock Dry Dock having her propellers repaired. In 1974 she was sold to the Greek ship owner Michael Karageorgis and renamed *Navarino*. For the past 20 years she has suffered a series of mishaps and is currently laid up at Tampa, Florida. (IS)

After an active career of only 17 years the record-breaker *United States* (1952/53,329 grt) has been laid up for the past 31 years. Capable of speeds in excess of 38 knots, her only visit to Cape Town was on February 8, 1969, her final year of service. (IS)

At the end of World War Two the liner fleet of the Portuguese company Companhia Colonial consisted mainly of ex-German ships built during the first decade of the century. As part of their replacement programme a pair of three-class passenger ships were ordered from the Clyde shipbuilder, John Brown - *Pátria* (1947/13,196 grt) and *Império* (1948/13,186 grt) operated on the Portugal-Moçambique service until they were broken up in Taiwan in the early 1970s. (IS)

Another former colonial workhorse was Messageries Maritimes's *Jean Laborde* (1953/10,902 grt) which was sold to Epirotiki Line in 1976 as *Oceanos*. Here she is leaving Cape Town shortly before she was involved in one of the most spectacular sea rescues of the 20th century. After flooding in her engine room off the eastern coast of South Africa she started to sink - with the aid of South African Defence Force helicopters all 580 passengers and crew were saved before the ship sank on August 4, 1991. (IS)

When *Port Auckland* (11,945 grt) and her Swan, Hunter-built sister *Port Brisbane* were completed in 1949 they generated a huge amount of interest because of their modern design and complete contrast to the rather dowdy looking British cargo liners of the day. With a long forecastle, streamlined bridge front and funnel, they created an unique image for Port Line on the Australian and New Zealand run and looked like small passenger liners even though they only carried 12 passengers. In 1976 *Port Auckland* was converted into a sheep carrier *Mashaalah* for service between Australia and the Middle East and three years later was scrapped at Kaohsiung, Taiwan. (IS)

Ellerman Lines *City of Melbourne* (1959/9,914 grt) was also designed for the Australian run and was an innovative general and refrigerated cargo liner with engines and superstructure three-quarters aft. At the time of completion her main Sulzer-type oil engine was also among the most powerful in the world. With the advent of refrigerated container ships on the Australian service she was transferred to the UK-South African route. Renamed *City of Cape Town*, she was broken up in 1979. (IS)

During the 1960s many of the United States cargo lines started to replace their Second World War-built standard ships with new tonnage. *Margaret Lykes* (1963/9,927 grt) was one of a large group of cargo ships built for the New Orleans-based Lykes Lines which had been trading with South Africa since 1939 - these ships had a distinctive profile with split superstructure and twin stovepipe funnels. Like most American cargo ships, *Margaret Lykes* was heavily subsidised and in 1985 she was sold to the U.S. Department of Transport and renamed *Cape Carthage*. (IS)

In 1957 Moore-McCormack Lines of New York acquired Robin Line and before long their yellow and green funnels were a familiar sight in South African waters. The turbine-driven *Mormacsaga* (1962/12,724 grt) had this name between 1977 and 1983 but had been completed as *M.M. Dant* for the States Steamship Company. Moore-McCormack was taken over by United States Lines in the early 1980s. Shortly before the collapse of this famous U.S. company in 1986 *Mormacsaga*, now *American Saga*, also ended up in U.S. Department of Transport ownership as *Mormac Saga*. (IS)

The origins of the Cardiff tramp firm Reardon Smith Line went back to 1905 and at the end of World War Two the company had a fleet of seventeen ships. In 1950 their first post-war new vessels were completed by William Doxford and Sons, Sunderland - the 5,593 grt-motorships *King City* and *Queen City*. Both were sold in 1966 - *King City* to a Greek concern, which renamed her *Panagiotis Xilas*. She went to Spanish breakers in 1978. (IS)

In 1947 the South African Marine Corporation (Safmarine) took delivery of its first ship, the U.S. standard type Victory ship *New Bern Victory* (1945/7,607 grt). Renamed *Constantia* she inaugurated Safmarine's South Africa-USA service. In 1961 she became *South African Vanguard* which was later shortened to *S. A. Vanguard*. Sold out of the fleet in 1969, three years later she capsized and sank off Karachi with a cargo of wheat. (IS)

Cirrus (1950/7,796 grt) was one of four fast cargo ships, all named after cloud formations, built between 1947 and 1950 for the Swedish firm Rederi A/B Transatlantic. This beautiful ship carried a dozen passengers and was capable of a service speed of 19.5 knots - on a number of occasions she won the unofficial annual race to Europe with Australian wool. Always immaculate, she was sold to Greek owners in 1976 and was broken up in 1982. (IS)

Leaving the Victoria Basin in the 1960s, this old Dutch-built tramp was built in 1918 as *Nieuwe Maas* (3,781 grt). In 1930 she was bought by a German concern and renamed *Poseidon*. Handed to the Greek Government as a war reparation she was sold in 1948 and became *Maiotis*. In 1961 as *Evangelos* she was owned by a company in the Nomikos group and flew the Lebanese flag. Aged 51 she was sold to Pakistani breakers in 1969. (IS)

In 1966 the three major South African coasting lines merged their resources to form Unicorn Shipping Lines - one of these was African Coasters which had owned thirty one ships of which only three had been built for the company - the Scottish-built *Voorspeler* (1965/854 grt) was the last of these and the final vessel to join the fleet. In 1981, she was sold to Panamanian owners and renamed *Sagar*. For most of the 1980s, she was laid up in Bangladesh and was scrapped in 1988. (IS)

African Coasters' great rival was the Durban-based Smith's Coasters. In the 1930s this company ordered two ships from Scott & Sons, Glasgow especially for the South African coastal sugar trade - *Gamtoos* (1937/797 grt) and *Nahoon* (1936/788 grt). In 1942 *Gamtoos* was taken over by the Seaward Defence Force, converted into a floating workshop and salvage ship, and sent to the Mediterranean where she spent the next three years clearing wrecks. Her commander Lieutenant-Commander (later Admiral) Biermann was awarded the OBE for *Gamtoos*'s clearance of the graving dock at La Ciotat. On her return home in 1946 she remained in government service as a guano carrier from the barren West Coast Islands to Cape Town. The last coal-fired South African coaster, she was sunk by South African Air Force bombers off Robben Island in 1976 despite attempts to have her preserved as a national monument. (IS)

Blue Anchor and White Star

The Danish born Wilhelm Lund built up a successful emigrant service to Australia with his line which was incorporated into a limited company in 1904 as the Blue Anchor Line Ltd. In the same year, the company's largest ship was completed on the Clyde - *Geelong* (7,951 grt). In 1908 an even larger ship was built, the 9,339 grt *Waratah*, which mysteriously disappeared in 1909 on a voyage from Durban to Cape Town. Blue Anchor never recovered from this tragedy and shortly afterwards the fleet was taken over by P&O. On New Years Day 1916 *Geelong* sank north of Alexandria after a collision with the British cargo ship *Bonvilston* (1893/2,866 grt.) (ML)

White Star Line was another company, which was never the same after the loss of its flagship *Titanic* in 1912 - fifteen years later it was taken over by Lord Kylsant's Royal Mail Group. *Ionic* (1903/12,352 grt) was the last of three large passenger-refrigerated ships built by Harland and Wolff for the joint Shaw Savill & Albion-White Star service between England and Australia and New Zealand - note the flags on the main and mizzen masts. Following the merger of White Star with Cunard in 1934 *Ionic* was bought by Shaw Savill & Albion and was scrapped in 1937. (ML)

Clan Line

Run by the Cayzer family, Clan Line was one of the major cargo lines trading between Britain and South Africa. Services to the Cape commenced in 1881 and in 1956 Clan Line took over Union-Castle Line after two previous attempts ended in failure. After the formation of Clan Line Steamers Ltd. in 1890 the company expanded rapidly. *Clan Campbell* (1894/2,615 grt) was one of a group of six small freighters completed between 1891 and 1894 - note the stock-anchor and open bridge. Sold in 1914, she eventually ended up in Chinese hands and was destroyed in an air raid at Canton in December 1941. (ML)

The turret ship was a highly successful concept of cargo ship design. Most came from the Sunderland shipyard William Doxford and Sons and of the 182 built, 28 were completed for Clan Line. The main advantages of this type were safety and economy - the shape of the hull meant that bulk cargo such as grain was less likely to shift whilst having a standard hull type reduced the cost of building. The narrow deck also meant that Suez Canal dues, which were based on breadth of the upper deck, were lower. *Clan Stuart* (1900/3,594 grt) went aground at Simon's Town on November 21, 1914 - the tops of the engine cylinders can still be seen. Another Clan turret ship *Clan Monroe* (1897/4,853 grt) was wrecked on the opposite side of the Cape Peninsula at Slangkop in 1905. (ML)

During World War Two Clan Line lost 30 ships and *Clan Shaw* (1950/8,101 grt) was the first of the S-class war replacement vessels and the first in the fleet with the distinctive cowl top funnel. Like most of the Clan Line ships built in the 1950s she came from the Cayzer-owned Greenock Dockyard. In 1960 she was transferred to Springbok Line, a short-lived British and Commonwealth venture, and renamed *Steenbok*. The following year she became Safmarine's *South African Seafarer*, later shortened to *S.A. Seafarer*. In the early hours of July 1, 1966, in stormy conditions, she ran aground opposite the Green Point Lighthouse - all her passengers and crew were rescued by helicopter and within hours the ship broke her back. (RP)

Argyllshire (1956/9,359 grt) and her sister *Ayrshire* (1957/9,424 grt) were the longest ships built for the company to that date and were designed for the Australian refrigerated and wool trade. Like many of the Clan ships of that era she also had substantial heavy lift capabilities and in 1964 carried a long 98-ton boiler from Birkenhead to Port Elizabeth. She was sold in 1975 and two years later was scrapped in Taiwan. (IS)

Ellerman Lines

Like Charles Cayzer and Clan Line, John Reeves Ellerman was a highly successful ship owner who built up his empire through the acquisition of well known shipping companies which operated under the Ellerman Lines umbrella - one of these was Bucknall Steamship Lines which was taken over in 1908. The black funnel with white diamond shapes, also known as "Bucknall's teeth", had been a familiar sight in South Africa since 1891 and in 1914 the company was renamed Ellerman & Bucknall Steamship Co. Ltd. *Karroo* (1913/6,064 grt) was one of a pair of cargo ships built just before World War One. At the outbreak of war she was in Australia and was requisitioned as an army transport to carry troops to Europe. During her war service she had a number of close shaves with German submarines and as a result, some of her senior officers received awards for gallantry. Renamed *City of Khartoum* in 1927 she was scrapped in 1936 as part of the British Government "Scrap and Build" scheme. (ML)

George Smith & Sons' City Line was another company taken over by Ellerman and *City of Venice* (1924/8,762 grt) was completed for the line's Calcutta-New York passenger-cargo service. Seen here in Bucknall colours she was fitted with quadruple expansion engines and had a service speed of 14 knots. On July 4, 1943, whilst on convoy in the Mediterranean, she was torpedoed and sunk by the German submarine *U 375* with the loss of at least 11 lives. (ML)

At the end of World War One, like many German shipping companies, DDG Hansa, Bremen had to surrender all its ships to the allies as war reparations. These included the newly completed *Geierfels* (1919/7,501 grt) which was bought by City Line in 1921 and renamed *City of Bagdad*. By a strange quirk of fate, on July 11, 1940 she was captured in the Indian Ocean by another former DDG Hansa ship - the infamous German raider *Atlantis* (ex *Goldenfels* 1937/7,862 grt). Most of her crew were taken captive and the ship was sunk with explosives. (ML)

One of the great tragedies in World War Two was the loss of this attractive two-funnelled liner - *City of Benares* (1936/11,081 grt) which was built for City Lines' India passenger-cargo service. Here she is entering Duncan Dock in wartime grey on August 1, 1940. Six weeks later, she left Liverpool in a convoy bound for Montreal with 191 passengers including 90 children being evacuated to Canada. On September 17, she was torpedoed in the Atlantic by the German submarine *U 48* and sank. Many lifeboats were swamped in heavy seas and although survivors were rescued during the next few days a total of 258 lives were lost including 77 children. Following this disaster, the evacuation of children abroad ceased. (JM)

Dutch connections

As a former Dutch colony South Africa has always had strong links with the Netherlands and in 1919 the government-subsidised Netherlands South Africa Steamship Company started a cargo-passenger service between Holland and South Africa - their ships featuring -*fontein* (fountain) names. In 1932 the company was taken over by the United Netherlands Company's Holland East Africa Line which had ships names ending in -*kerk* (church) - the new concern became Holland Afrika Lijn.

In 1934 a pair of 10,000 grt-passenger ships was delivered with -*fontein* names and curved maierform bows - the success of these ships led to an order in the late 1930s for three slightly larger versions with traditional bows. The first, *Klipfontein* (10,544 grt), was finished in 1939 by the Smit yard, Rotterdam which also built the second in the series, *Oranjefontein* (10,549 grt) completed at the end of 1940. In March the following year, *Oranjefontein* was seized by the German Navy and was later used as a transport. At war's end she was taken from Kiel to Newcastle and refitted. After a voyage to the Dutch East Indies she made her maiden trip to South Africa and is seen in this extraordinary wide-angle photograph by Terrence McNally arriving in Table Bay for the first time in April 1946. In 1967 she was sold to Spanish breakers. (JM)

The final ship in the trio, *Jagersfontein* (10,574 grt), was built by Schichau, Danzig. Launched in 1940 as *Elandsfontein* she too was taken over by the German Navy although incomplete. In 1945 she was damaged by artillery fire and sank - two years later the wreck was raised and towed to Vlissingen for completion. Renamed *Jagersfontein*, she entered service in March 1950 - a popular liner, she was also sold for scrap in 1967. (RP)

Most of the United Netherlands's cargo ships had -*kerk* names and after World War Two the company purchased a number of U.S. standard type vessels including seven Victory ships - *Grootekerk* (7,647 grt) was built at Portland, Oregon in 1945 as *Gonzaga Victory* and came under the Dutch flag in 1946 until her sale to a Chinese scrap yard in 1970, the year United Netherlands merged with a number of Dutch firms to form Nedlloyd. (RP)

Amerskerk (1952/8,583 grt) was a one-off cargo ship built by the Hamburg yard Howaldtswerke. Turbine-driven, she had numerous masts and space for 72 passengers (reduced to 12 in 1968). Sold out of the fleet in 1972, she was scrapped in 1973. (GA)

Among the most evocative liners which visited Cape Town in the 1950s were those belonging to Koninklijke Java-China-Paketvaart Lijnen, more commonly known as Royal Interocean Lines. These ships operated from the Far East to South America and the flagships were the trio completed in 1938 for Koninklijke Paketvaart-Maatschappij (K.P.M.).

Named after the founders of K.P.M. they were: *Ruys* (14,155 grt) - shown above pre-war in K.P.M. colours (ML), *Tegelberg* (14,150 grt) - left (GA) and *Boissevain* (14,134 grt) - opposite top (GA). They all had excellent passenger accommodation and were used as troopships during the war - in 1968 they were sent to Taiwanese breakers.

The smaller *Tjitjalengka* (10,972 grt) was built in 1939 for the Dutch East Indies-Far East passenger service and for much of the war was a hospital ship. In 1959 she was driven ashore during a typhoon in Japan and was refloated three months later. She too went for scrap in 1968. (IS)

an der Hagen (1958/5,924 grt) was one of four small andsome freighters built for RIL in the late 1950s - the teriors of these ships were excellent for both officers d the dozen passengers. Renamed *Straat Lagos* in 1967 e was sold in 1978. As *Chai Trader* she was demolished 1984. (GA)

Farrell Lines

Bought in 1926 by the Farrell Brothers, the American South African Line operated the longest non-stop ocean crossing in the world - 6,795 miles from New York to Cape Town. The first cargo-passenger ship built for the new owners was the twin-screw *City of New York* (1930/8,272 grt). Diesel-powered, which was unusual for an American-built vessel, she carried 60 passengers and did not have a sister ship. On March 29, 1942 she was torpedoed by the German submarine *U 160* near Cape Hatteras and sank with the loss of 26 passengers and crew. (ML)

In 1948 American South African Line was renamed Farrell Lines. Keen to rebuild their passenger service between New York and Cape Town, the company bought two former 1940-built Delta Line passenger-cargo ships, *Delbrasil* and *Deltargentino*, which after refurbishment emerged in 1949 as the 7,922 grt-*African Endeavor* - seen leaving the Victoria Basin - and *African Enterprise*. With a passenger capacity of 86, *African Endeavor* and her sister were seldom full, and incurred a great loss for Farrell Lines. After only ten years on the run, both vessels were withdrawn and laid up in the James River, until scrapped in 1969 at Baltimore - their place of birth. (GA)

African Comet (1962/11,350 grt) was the first of a series of six high speed cargo liners designed to cut the New York-Cape Town run from 18 to 14 days - turbine driven, they were capable of a speed in excess of 20 knots. Withdrawn in 1980 she was sold to the U.S. Department of Transport and renamed *Cape Alava*. (RP)

Robin Line

Farrell's great competitor on the New York service was the Seas Shipping Corporation - known as Robin Line, their rival monthly service started in 1935 with four fifteen year-old ships with -Robin names, two of which were lost during World War Two and a third used in the Normandy breakwaters. Robin had the Chrysler and Ford contracts and here *Robin Gray* (1920/6,896 grt) is offloading wooden crates with Chrysler cars in 1937 - note the rickety wooden ladder and stowage conditions compared with the container ships of today. (JM)

The post-war Robin fleet consisted of twelve freighters built during the war. These ships had a distinctive design with a long raised forecastle and dummy funnel with a single stovepipe. The passenger accommodation for twelve was also of a very high standard. In 1957 another New York company, Moore-McCormack Lines, acquired Robin Line and the ships continued to trade until the late 1960s. Here *Robin Locksley* (1941/8,024 grt) is entering port having being towed by the brand-new Cape Town harbour tug *Danie Hugo* (1959/812 grt) following an engine breakdown 90 miles from Cape Town. Laid up in 1969 *Robin Locksley* was scrapped a year later. (RP)

Japanese emigrant carriers

For almost a quarter of a century, Osaka Shosen Kaisha (O.S.K.) operated a unique round-the-world service from Japan to South America around the Cape of Good Hope, returning to Japan via Panama and Los Angeles. Outbound, the ships carried emigrants to Brazil (Brazil has the largest Japanese community outside Japan and the USA) and on the return journey, various cargoes were picked up en route including raw cotton, Japan being at that time the world's major textile producer. *Arabia Maru* (1919/9,480 grt) was one of five large Japanese-built passenger and cargo ships completed for O.S.K. - over 300 emigrants were accommodated in dormitories on the main deck. In World War Two *Arabia Maru* became a naval transport and as such was torpedoed by the U.S. submarine *Bluegill* near Manila in October 1944.

Argentina Maru (1939/12,755 grt) and her sister *Brazil Maru* (1939/12,752 grt), with their streamlined appearance, were the epitome of 1930s modern style and engineering. Although they were essentially state subsidised emigrant ships, first class passengers had the use of fine facilities on the three upper decks, including swimming pool, nursery, gymnasium and well lit lounges and dining room. *Argentina Maru* made only four voyages before the attack on Pearl Harbour. From 1942 to 1943 she was converted into the aircraft carrier *Kaiyo* and in July 1945 hit a mine and was damaged beyond repair. The South African Maritime Museum, next to the Robinson Graving Dock, has a magnificent model of this ship. (AD)

Deutsche Ost-Afrika-Linie

The red, white and black colours of the first German national flag, on a yellow background, with black top are one of the most distinctive funnel markings ever designed and have been on the ships of the Deutsche Ost-Afrika-Linie (DOAL) for over 110 years. The company was founded by the Woermann family in 1890 initially to serve the recently acquired German territories in East Africa. Woermann-Linie had by then been set up with ships mainly bearing the name of a *Woermann* or *Bohlen* (relations by marriage) family member, with funnels featuring the green, white and blue colours of the company - these vessels traded on the west coast of Africa and included *Gertud Woermann* (1885/1,743 grt) - leaving Cape Town for the final time in August 1903 - nineteen days later she was wrecked near Port Nolloth. Another *Gertud Woermann* was bought as a replacement in 1904 and she too was wrecked a few months after entering service. (ML)

The pre World War One years saw the development of the archetypal German Africa liner, with open decks, combined bridge and poop deck, short well deck forward, long forecastle, and a relatively high superstructure, surmounted by a large funnel which gave the impression of a much bigger vessel - the ships were mainly named after key positions of German leadership e.g. *Gouverneur*, *General*, *König*, etc., carried three classes, and were very popular especially for First Class travellers. *Prinzregent* (1903/6,341 grt) served on the round Africa service and after the war was ceded to France as war reparations. As *Cordoba* she operated on the Marseilles-South America run for S.G.T.M. until 1932 when she went to Italian breakers. (ML)

After losing almost its entire fleet of 74 ships at the conclusion of World War One, DOAL set about a replacement programme and between 1921 and 1928 a dozen new liners were completed including a pair of two-funnelled passenger ships -*Watussi* (1928/9,552 grt.) and *Ubena* (1928/9,554 grt.). In December 1939 under the guise of an Union-Castle liner, *Watussi* attempted to make a dash for South America via the Cape but was spotted by a South African Air Force aircraft just south of Cape Point and ordered to Simon's Town. Her crew set fire to the ship which later sank - here she is ablaze, her forward funnel painted in Union-Castle red and black whilst the fire has revealed the DOAL colours on her aft funnel. (JM)

How times have changed. A labour intensive dockside scene in the 1960s with a small DOAL 4,966 grt-cargoship, either the 1956-built *Ubena* or *Usaramo* (GA), and the 52,682 grt-containership *DAL Kalahari* (1977) which can carry almost 3,000 container units at a service speed of 20 knots. (IS)

Scandinavian traders

Scandinavian-owned ships were usually the most immaculate of all those which called at Cape Town - none more so than the white ships of Thor Dahl's Christensen's Canadian African Line. Ironically this Norwegian company owed its origin to one of the filthiest trades - whaling - hence the whale trade mark on the funnel and company logo. All the ships also featured the god Thor on the bow as we can see on *Thorscarrier* (1959/8,742 grt) arriving on her maiden voyage from Canada in 1959. In 1968 she was sold to Norwegian America Line and renamed *Vindafjord* and ten years later was bought by a Greek company. As *Nordave*, she ran ashore in Pakistan in 1979 and was declared a constructive total loss. (AN)

Elgaren (1957/5,737 grt) belonged to the Swedish company Rederi A/B Transatlantic and like all the ships in the fleet was always in beautiful condition with painted decks and excellent accommodation for 12 passengers. In 1975 she was bought by the Shipping Corporation of Saudi Arabia and renamed *Arab Alhijaz* - in 1983 she went to Pakistani breakers. (GA)

Tai Yang (1929/7,084) was the first of ten large motorships completed for the Norwegian Wilhelm Wilhelmsen Line for trade between New York and the Far East - hence the Chinese name. Six of these ships with split superstructure, straight stem and counter stern survived World War Two and lasted with the company for at least thirty years. *Tai Yang* was sold in 1962 to a Lebanese firm and renamed *Mousse*. She was only broken up in 1970 aged forty-one. (RP)

Natal (1914/4,171 grt) was one of five ships with South African names which were completed in 1914 for the Danish East Asiatic Company and then transferred the following year to a new Danish East Asiatic tramp subsidiary D/S A/S Orient. Sold in 1930, *Natal* became the Swedish-owned *Brage* and in 1934 she was sold to a Finnish company and renamed *Orient*. In July 1944 whilst in a German convoy she was torpedoed and sunk by British aircraft south of Helgoland. (ML)

Portuguese and Italians

The small Portuguese liner *Portugal* (1899/3,998 grt) inaugurated Empreza Nacional de Navegação's regular service between Portugal and Moçambique in 1906. In 1918 Empreza Nacional was liquidated and a new concern formed - Companhia Nacional de Navegação whose former flagship, *Principe Perfeito* (1961/19,393 grt), still exists and is laid up in Greece as *Marianna IX*. *Portugal* was scrapped in 1925. (ML)

Nacional's rival on the African run was Companhia Colonial and in the late 1940s two new 800-capacity passenger liners were completed - *Império* (1948/13,186 grt) and *Pátria* (1947/13,196 grt) - the latter is shown on page 67. In 1961 they were joined by *Infante Dom Henrique* (23,306 grt) and for much of the latter part of the 1960s carried troops for the independence wars in Moçambique and Angola. With the end of colonial rule, all three were withdrawn from service in the early 1970s. (IS)

Between 1951 and 1953 Lloyd Triestino took delivery of seven new Italian-built liners. Three were for the Genoa-Australia service, two for Genoa-Hong Kong and a pair for the Genoa-Cape Town route - *Africa* (1952/11,427 grt) and *Europa* (1952/11,430 grt). Painted white, these handsome passenger ships with their goalpost masts forward and bipod signal mast above the bridge always kept their modern look right up to the mid 1970s when they were retired because of fuel costs and the increased use of air travel. These liners were diesel-powered - *Africa* had Sulzer-type and *Europa* FIAT engines - and capable of a maximum speed of 21.5 knots. *Africa* was scrapped in 1980. (GA)

One of the 1950s septet still operates and is a regular caller at Cape Town. *Anastasis* (1953/11,701/53) was the former Far East liner *Victoria*. Owned by Mercy Ships, a Christian charity organisation which provides medical help to third world countries, *Anastasis* is run by dedicated volunteers and is little changed since her Lloyd Triestino days either inside or externally. (AI)

Red Peril

In the 1950s the greatest evil for the South African Nationalist Government was the threat of Communism and nothing illustrated this better than the paranoia over the visit of the Russian Navy training ship *Tovarisch* (1933/1,392 grt) with 139 cadets in October 1957. Berthed on Eastern Mole, one of the remotest parts of the harbour, visitors were prevented from visiting the ship by the harbour police and the local newspaper came out with a banner headline *Russian ship behind city iron curtain*. *Tovarisch* was built as the German training ship *Gorch Foch* and recently was under arrest for a long period in England because of her poor condition. (GA)

Despite the anti-Russian sentiment of the South African authorities, Russian ships were seen every year in the Victoria Basin carrying scientists to Antarctica. Here is *Ob* (1954/7,503 grt) showing her ice-breaker bow. Named after an Arctic river, she was one of six Dutch-built Russian ships designed for polar service and rescued the Japanese research vessel *Soya* when she became trapped in ice. (GA)

This George Aschman photograph shows the crew of *Ob*'s sistership, *Lena*, which was also completed in 1954. Despite language difficulties I visited a number of these ships in the late 1950s and found the Russians to be the most hospitable of all the nationalities I came across.

Since the break-up of the Soviet Union many of the state-owned companies have experienced great difficulties. The cruise liner *Odessa* (1966/20,027), seen leaving Cape Town in immaculate condition, has been languishing under arrest for the past five years at Naples and looks a very sorry sight now. (IS)

Tankers

Despite all the negative publicity whenever they are wrecked, tankers remain a vital link in the energy chain. In the early days of the industry, oil was shipped in barrels and this remains the main measure for oil production. At the beginning of the 20th century oil was progressively transported in specially designed engines-aft tankers although for many remote parts of the world petroleum products were carried in tin cans placed in wooden boxes for protection, and conveyed in cargo ships. *Physa* (1904/3,899 grt) was a case-oil carrier for the Anglo-Saxon Petroleum Company later known as Shell - completed as *Saint Egbert*, she was bought by Anglo-Saxon in 1917 and disposed of in the early 1930s. (ML)

The 1950s saw a rapid growth in the size of oil tankers. Dwarfed by today's super tankers, *British Justice* (21,079 grt) was one of the largest tankers in the giant B. P. Tanker fleet of 1957. Sold in 1973 to Greek owners she was briefly *Salamis* before being broken up in 1976. (AN)

The pioneer for large tankers was undoubtedly the American ship-owner Daniel Ludwig whose tankers in the late 1950s were the largest in the world. Many of them had their annual refit in Cape Town's giant Sturrock Dry Dock, including *Universe Commander* (1957/51,398 grt) - this view was taken looking forward to the rather austere bridge section. (PN)

The problems with stress from rough seas on giant crude oil carriers was graphically illustrated in June 1994 when the Iranian tanker *Tochal* (1977/ 144,688 grt) lost most of her bow 90 miles north west of Cape Town. The damage was too great for repair and she was towed for scrap later that year. (IS)

In 1992 the most serious drought in living memory hit Southern Africa and the failure of the wheat and maize crops meant that 50% of South Africa's wheat had to be imported and for months ships offloaded grain in Cape Town. Here foodstuff is being transhipped from the tanker *Kittanning* (1977/44,875 grt) into the small bulk carrier *Europegasus* (1972/ 14,315 grt.) (PN)

Whaling

It is hard to condone modern whaling. Anyone who has seen these wonderful creatures surfacing at close range, will find it difficult to imagine that for the first three-quarters of the 20th century, 1.3 million were slaughtered in the Antarctic alone. With increasingly larger factory ships and more efficient catchers, most species of large whales would probably be extinct by now, had it not been for the intervention of the international community. Norway has always been at the forefront of whaling since the invention by Tønsberg's Svend Foyn of a gun that launched harpoons containing an explosive charge. Pre-World War One Norwegian whale catchers were tiny like *Durbana* (1911/131 grt) - note the limited amount of freeboard. In later years she became the French trawler *Bordagain*. (ML)

In the 1950s the whaling fleet would call at Cape Town in spring before leaving for Antarctic waters. Here are three 1951-built catchers of just over 600 grt belonging to the Anders Jahre fleet. At the top of the foremast is the crow's nest for spotting whales whilst the walkway from the bridge to the bow allowed quick access to the harpoon gun. When the factory ships returned to Europe at the end of each season, many of these catchers spent the winter laid up in Cape Town. (GA)

Despite their involvement in the manufacture of margarine, the Dutch did not get seriously into the whaling business until after the war, when in 1946, the Nederlandsche Maatschappij Voor De Walvischvaart N.V. (Vinke and Co.) of Amsterdam bought a tanker and converted her into the factory ship *Willem Barendsz* (1931/15,500 grt). In 1955 they took delivery of a new *Willem Barendsz* (26,830 grt) which at the time was the largest whale factory ship in the world. In 1965, her name unchanged, she was bought by a Cape Town concern and used as a fish factory ship until 1973 when she was sold to Korean owners. As *Ocean Pioneer* she continues to operate for the Korean fishing industry. (GA)

The Vinke catchers were mainly steam-driven converted corvettes until the late 1950s when three new ships were ordered - two with diesel-power and the third, the world's first gas turbine-driven catcher. Here is one of the new diesel catchers *Thomas W. Vinke* (658 grt) leaving the Victoria Basin on a press trip in November 1959. She was later sold to Thor Dahl and became *Thordr*. (AN)

Wooden fishing boats and old coasters

From the days of Rogge Bay at the foot of Adderley Street, the small wooden fishing boats of Cape Town have always been an integral part of Cape Town life. Now they have been banished to make way for even more corporate offices as the developers continue to ruin what little is left of the old harbour. This photograph from the 1960s shows what the fishing harbour next to the Collier Jetty looked like until a few years ago. (GA)

On Sunday afternoon nothing used to happen in the Victoria Basin! The coaster in the background - *Induna* (1938, 1,214 grt) had a very interesting career and was twice sunk in the war when German-owned and ran for Smiths Coasters from 1954 to 1962. (AN)

The oldest of all the South African coastal companies was the Thesen Steamship Company whose ships bearing a black funnel with red band and white star were a familiar sight for over seventy years. The company was founded by the Norwegian Thesen family who in 1870 settled in Knysna, a small port between Cape Town and Port Elizabeth. Knysna owed its existence to large local indigenous forests, and Thesens soon dominated the timber trade. *Karatara* (1882/540 grt) was already 31 years old when Thesens bought her from Norwegian owners in 1913. In May 1921 whilst on a voyage from Cape Town to East London with a cargo which included case-oil she caught fire and was abandoned - towed to Cape Town her hull was incorporated into a jetty at Saldanha Bay. (ML)

African Coasters' *Bulwark* (1920/1,374 grt) was not a lucky ship. Built as *Mahmoudieh* for the Khedivial Mail Steamship Co, London - in 1943, as *Finland* she was beached in the River Tagus after a collision with a Portuguese steamer - refloated, she was repaired in Lisbon. In 1955 she was bought by African Coasters as *Bulwark* but like so many South African coasters, her career came to an abrupt end when she was wrecked in 1963 near Danger Point. *HMS Birkenhead* foundered nearby in 1852 with the loss of 445 lives, but fortunately for those on *Bulwark*, all were saved.

The Suez Crises of 1956-1957 and 1967-1975

The closure of the Suez Canal during the two Arab-Israeli Wars was another great time for ship buffs in Cape Town with the harbour always full and shi waiting in the Bay for a berth. In this Robert Pabst photograph taken during the second Suez Canal closure, every berth in Duncan Dock has been taken wi a long line of ships from Swedish Rederi A/B Transatlantic's *Alabama* (1962/5,979 grt) to the Chandris passenger liner *Australis* (1940/26,315 grt).

Orsova (1954/28,790 grt) was the final ship in a trio of post-war passenger liners built by Vickers-Armstrongs Ltd., Barrow-in-Furness for Orient Line's London-Australia service. Her sisters were *Oronsay* and *Orcades* and all three had a unique profile with a single streamlined funnel and bridge practically amidships - the "Welsh hat" on her funnel helped with problems of soot on deck. *Orsova* can be immediately recognised because she was the only one without a signal mast above the bridge. With the increase in air travel and fuel costs they were sold to Taiwanese breakers in the early 1970s. (RP)

With a silver-grey hull and black funnels, *Willem Ruys* (21,119 grt) was the famous flagship of Rotterdam Lloyd. Although she was laid down in 1939 at the Dutch shipyard De Schelde, work was constantly interrupted by resistance groups after the German invasion of Holland and she was only completed in 1947. Designed for the Holland-Indonesia run she was later transferred to the Australia service. In 1964 she was sold to the Italian shipowner Achille Lauro and given his name. As *Achille Lauro* (see front cover) she became infamous when she was hijacked in 1985 by Arab terrorists and in November1994 she caught fire off the Horn of Africa and sank. (GA)

Johan van Oldenbarnevelt (19,040 grt) also ended her days on fire. She was completed for Rotterdam Lloyd's rival Stoomvaart Maatschappij "Nederland" in 1930. In the 1950s she had a Dutch government contract to carry emigrants to Australia - up to 1,400 passengers were accommodated mainly in large dormitories. She is seen here in the Duncan Dock with Dutch and Indonesian passengers taking a stroll during the first Suez Crisis. In 1963 she was bought by Greek Line for use as a cruise liner and renamed *Lakonia*. On December 19, 1963 she left Southampton fully booked on a Christmas cruise and three days later caught fire north of Madeira with the tragic loss of 128 lives - she later sank under tow. (GA)

Bows

With the advances of naval architecture and shipbuilding technology, the shape of the bow has varied considerably over the years. Here we have the functional straight stem of a late 19th century British tramp steamer - *Cumeria* (1893/3,101 grt) in the Robinson Graving Dock whilst on charter to Bucknall Steamship Lines. In 1906 she was sold to an Italian company and renamed *Luigino Accame* - demolition took place in 1924 at Genoa after a period of being laid up. (ML)

The great leap forward in Union-Castle mailship design came about in the late 1930s with the introduction of three fast large passenger motorships. *Capetown Castle* (1938.27,000 grt) was the last in the trio to be completed by Harland and Wolff and spent her entire 29 year-career with Union-Castle. Here she is flying the Blue Peter at B-berth - note the rat guards at the top of the mooring rope. (GA)

The Liberty Ship was the ultimate in prefabrication. With welded hulls these ships were built in remarkably fast times and one vessel, *Robert E. Peary*, was launched in November 1942 only 4 days, 15.5 hours after her keel was laid. The Liberty Ship shown here was completed in April 1945 as *Elwin F. Knowles*. Before she was broken up in 1968 she had seven different names including *Zuider Zee* (7,212 grt) from 1955 to 1961. (GA)

The wonderful flared bow of Holland America Line's passenger liner *Statendam* (1957/24,294 grt) during a cruise in the late 1950s. Often overshadowed by her larger running mate *Rotterdam* which was completed in 1959, *Statendam* was a handsome looking ship and has remained laid up in Greece as *Regent Star* ever since the collapse of Regency Cruises in 1995. (GA)

Funnels

The variety of funnel designs is inexhaustible - here is a selection of funnel photographs taken by me as a teenager in the late 1950s and early 1960s. This tall buff-coloured funnel belonged to Orient Line's two-funnelled passenger liner *Orontes* (1929/19,970 grt) on her last call at Cape Town in 1961 a year before she was sent to the breakers - note the large ventilators and stays attached to the funnel.

No hard hats for these sailors painting the funnel on Cunard Line's *Caronia* (1948/34,183 grt) during her 1959 World Cruise. When completed, her funnel was claimed to be the largest ever fitted on a ship and bigger than those on the *Queen Elizabeth*.

Poor *Dominion Monarch* (1939/26,463 grt). She was designed for Shaw Savill and Albion to carry 517 passengers to Australia and New Zealand in first class only. Unfortunately she was completed just before the outbreak of the Second World War and when she returned to service in 1948 the social order had changed and in 1962 she was replaced by the 1,412-capacity tourist class liner *Northern Star* (24,733 grt).

General Le Roy Eltinge (13,100 grt) was built in 1945 as a troopship for the US Navy. One of a large group of C4-type standard ships with engines aft she was able to carry over 3,000 troops. Sold in 1969 and converted into a container ship, she was demolished in 1980.

Canadian Pacific's *Empress of Britain* (1956/25,516 grt) made a number of cruises in the early 1960s before being sold to Greek Line in 1964. In 1975 she was bought by Carnival Cruise Lines as one of their first cruise ships - *Carnivale*. She now operates for Thomson Cruises as *Topaz*.

Rotterdam (1959/38,645 grt) made her first call at Cape Town in March 1960 and I was privileged to have dinner aboard what was then, and for many years hence, one of the world's most prestigious cruiseships. Sold to Premier Cruises in 1997 and renamed *Rembrandt*, she catered for the low fare cruise market until the recent bankruptcy of Premier.

Cruise ships

Although cruise ships had started in a limited way before World War One to the Mediterranean and Norway, cruising took off in the mid 1920s when many of the lines recognised the opportunities which existed for off-season cruising. In 1922 American Express chartered Cunard Line's brand-new *Laconia* (1922/19,680 grt) - seen here in the 1930s - for the first ever world cruise by a passenger liner - that voyage was via the Suez Canal. Regular calls by cruise ships at Cape Town started in February 1926 with the Royal Mail liner *Orca* (1918/16,063 grt) and she was soon followed by other transatlantic liners. In September 1942, with 2,732 people on board, including 1,800 Italian prisoners-of-war, *Laconia* was torpedoed and sunk in the South Atlantic by the German submarine *U 156*. Attempts by the submarine to rescue survivors were thwarted when it was fired at by a US bomber and as a result the German Navy command gave an instruction, the "Laconia Order", that in future U-boats should cease the practice of rescuing survivors from sunken ships.

One of the most famous and luxurious cruise ships in the 1930s was *Arandora Star* (1927/14,694 grt) - arriving in January 1935. The final ship in a group five built for Blue Star Line, she was converted into a full-time 354-capacity cruise ship in 1929 and was very successful. In May 1940 she too was torpede with prisoners-of-war aboard in the Atlantic with the loss of 761 lives. (JM)

One of the largest cruise ships in the 1930s was Canadian Pacific's *Empress of Britain* (1931/42,348 grt). In this evocative 1934 photograph by the late Ray Ryan *Empress of Britain* is arriving in the newly built Southern Basin on a beautiful calm early morning. When she was due to leave, a south-easterly gale kept her glued to the quay despite the frantic efforts of three powerful tugs. This south-easterly wind - known locally as the "Cape doctor" - is most prevalent in the summer months and hurtles over the top of Table Mountain, causing the famous cloud cover called the "table cloth" before hitting the city often with great intensity. The Achilles heel of the new basin was immediately apparent and it was realised that to deal with similar situations, new berths were needed in line with the south east - this was the start of a major expansion plan for the harbour which culminated in the completion of the Duncan Dock in 1943.

Empress of Britain returned to Cape Town during World War Two as a troopship and is seen leaving, painted grey, at the end of May 1940. Five months later she became Britain's largest war loss when she was attacked by a German bomber near Ireland. She caught fire and was taken in tow by a Polish destroyer but two days later was torpedoed by a German submarine and sank. (JM)

Elderly American passengers from Holland America Line's *Statendam* (1957/24,294) setting out on a local tour in the 1950s. (GA)

One of the most beautiful cruise ships ever built was *Bergensfjord* (18,739 grt), completed by Swan, Hunter for Norwegian America Line in 1956. Almost yacht-like in appearance, she was sold to French Line in 1971 as a temporary replacement for *Antilles* which had been lost by fire earlier that year. Renamed *De Grasse,* in 1973 she was bought by Norwegian interests for operation in the Far East. From then onwards her career took a slide until, as *Rasa Sayang*, she was destroyed by fire in Greece during a refit in 1980. (GA)

Here we have another view of *Caronia* - this time leaving in a howling south easter. By the mid-1960s the "Green Goddess" was looking rather dated and was expensive to run. Despite a major refurbishment of her accommodation in 1965, Cunard decided to sell the ship in 1968 and she was bought by a Panamanian company - after a refit in Greece she was renamed *Caribia*. In 1969 following an engine room explosion she arrived at New York and was laid up for almost five years. In 1974 she was being towed to breakers in Taiwan when she went aground at Guam and broke up. (RP)

In 1958 Moore-McCormack Lines took delivery of a pair of 14,984 grt-passenger ships which were the finest US-flagged liners of their day - *Argentina* (above) and *Brasil*. Both ships were sold to Holland America in 1971 and despite having had numerous names since then, their condition is very good - a credit to their builders Ingalls who are now constructing the largest passenger ship ever built in the United States. *Argentina* continues to operate for New Commodore Cruise Lines as *Enchanted Isle*. (GA)

Southern Cross (1955/20,204 grt) brought me to England in 1967. Among the first passenger ships with engines aft, this revolutionary ship was built by Harland and Wolff for Shaw Savill & Albion and their round-the-world service to Australia and New Zealand from Southampton. In 1973 she was sold to a Greek company and converted into the cruise ship *Calypso*. Little altered she currently cruises the Caribbean as *Oceanbreeze*. (RP)

After a short period in Cape Town I returned to the UK in 1970 aboard *Angelina Lauro* (24,377 grt) which like her running mate *Achille Lauro* was a former Dutch East Indies liner and was also lost through fire. Completed in 1939 as *Oranje* she was the flagship of Stoomvaart Maatschappij "Nederland" and for most of World War Two operated as an Australian hospital ship. In 1964 she was sold to Achille Lauro, renamed *Angelina Lauro* and rebuilt at Genoa. In 1979 she caught fire at St. Thomas and was declared a total loss. (RP)

The power of the sea - in December 1995 *Star Odyssey* (1972/28,668) arrived at Cape Town with her bow badly bent in an Indian Ocean storm. Built as *Royal Viking Star* she was one of a trio of sisters which were at one time the top cruise ships in the world. During the early 1980s all three were cut in half and lengthened by 91 feet. In 1996 she was sold to Fred. Olsen and is now the popular *Black Watch*. (IS)

Safmarine bought the German cruise ship *Astor* (1981/18,591 grt) in 1984 for a new South Africa-Southampton service. The venture was a failure and after only a year she was sold to Deutsche Seereederei and renamed *Arkona*. A second *Astor* was built in 1986 but she too was unsuccessful and was sold in 1988. (RP)

INDEX OF SHIP PHOTOGRAPHS

PHOTOGRAPHIC SOURCES

Every effort has been made to correctly attribute photographs used in the book. Any photograph not coded with one of the following codes is from the author's collection

AD Alex Duncan Collection; **AG** Ambrose Greenway Collection; **AI** Andrew Ingpen; **AN** Albert Newall; **CA** Cape Town Archives (codes: **DRJ** Dr. C.F.Juritz, **E** Arthur Elliott); **GA** George Aschman; **IS** Ian Shiffman (http://home.worldonline.co.za/~snai), **JM** John Marsh Collection, SA Maritime Museum (http://maritimemuseum.ac.za); **ML** Martin Leendertz Collection, SA Library; **PN** Peter Newall; **RP** Robert Pabst.